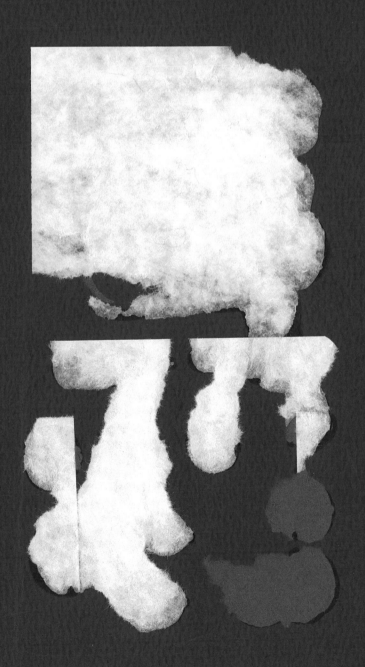

The Story of the
THREE WISE KINGS

The Story of the
THREE WISE KINGS

Retold & illustrated by

TOMIE dePAOLA

G. P. PUTNAM'S SONS

New York

To FLORENCE ALEXANDER,
a wonderful lady, a superb agent
and a very dear friend

Text and illustrations copyright © 1983 by Tomie dePaola.
All rights reserved. Published simultaneously in
Canada by General Publishing Co. Limited, Toronto.
Printed in the United States of America.
Library of Congress Cataloging in Publication Data
DePaola, Tomie.
The story of the Three Wise Kings.
Summary: Three wise men of the East, having seen a new star
symbolizing the birth of a great king, follow the star to
Bethlehem where they present gifts to the newborn Jesus.
1. Jesus Christ—Nativity—Juvenile literature.
2. Magi—Juvenile literature. [1. Jesus Christ—Nativity.
2. Magi. 3. Bible stories—N.T.] I. Title.
BT315.2.D46   1983   232.9'23   83-4609
ISBN 0-399-20998-0
ISBN 0-399-20999-9 (pbk.)
First impression.

A Word about the Kings

The first written word about the kings appears in the Gospel of St. Matthew. His brief account tells of wise men who went to Bethlehem to honor the child who would become King of the Jews. Matthew does not give them names nor does he say how many wise men there were. His only mention as to where they came from is that they followed a star from the East.

Over the centuries details about the wise men were added gradually. In the second century, they were transformed into kings and their number was determined. Early art from the period shows two and four figures, but three figures were used most often and persisted into later centuries because Matthew had referred to three gifts.

By the eighth century, each of the kings had a name, an area from which he came, and physical descriptions. Melchior of Arabia was depicted as an old man; Gaspar of Tharsis as young; and Balthazar of Saba was shown as mature and black.

The feast of the three kings, called the Feast of the Epiphany, is celebrated on January 6th, twelve days after Christmas. In some countries, this is the day on which gifts are given.

In this book, I have chosen to paint the mother and child in the traditional pose referred to as ''Seat of Wisdom, Throne of Justice.'' This pose was frequently used in Romanesque paintings of the Adoration of the Kings.

T.deP.   1983

Long ago in the East,
in lands far from one another,
there lived three kings—
Melchior of Arabia,
Gaspar of Tharsis,
and Balthazar of Saba.

These wise men studied the stars.

Each night,
they looked at the sky
and wrote down where the stars were,
where they had come from,
and where they were going.

One night,
a star they had never seen before
appeared in the sky.

Each of the kings consulted his books
and found that this new star was the sign
that a great king was about to be born.

So each king, not knowing about the others,
set out to follow the star,
to find the child-king
and to honor him.

And each carried with him a gift.
Melchior took gold;
Gaspar, frankincense;
and Balthazar, myrrh.

After many days and nights,
the three wise kings met.
They found that they were all following the same star
so they continued their journey together.

But as they came near to Jerusalem,
they lost sight of the star
and they did not know which way to go.

"Let us ask at the palace of King Herod,"
one of them said.
"Surely Herod will know of the birth
of another great king."

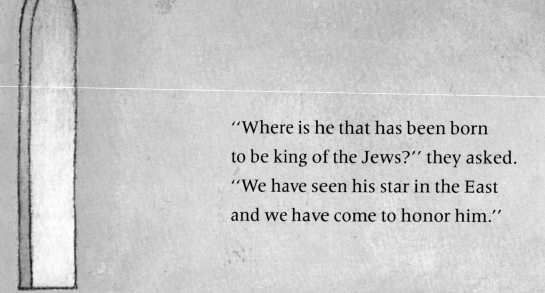

"Where is he that has been born
to be king of the Jews?" they asked.
"We have seen his star in the East
and we have come to honor him."

Now Herod, who was an evil man,
was disturbed when he heard this.
He wished to be
the only king in that land.
He went to his chief priests and learned men
and asked them where this child would be born.

"It has been written:
at Bethlehem in Judah,"
they told him.

Herod sent for the three kings.
''Go to Bethlehem
and find out all about the child-king,''
he said.
''And when you have found him,
come back and tell me
so I may worship him too.''

The three wise kings
set out for Bethlehem
not knowing that Herod wanted to destroy
the newborn baby.
And there in the sky,
once again, was the star.

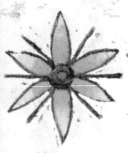

They followed it
until it stopped over the place
where the child was born.

Like a flame of fire
that star pointed out God,
the King of Kings.

And going into the place,
they saw the child with his mother, Mary,
and falling down on their knees they honored him.
Then, they opened their treasures
and offered the gifts
of gold and frankincense and myrrh.

That night as the kings slept,
they were warned in a dream
not to go back to Herod,
for he wished to destroy the child.

So the three kings,
to keep Herod from finding the child,
returned to their countries
by a different way.